Disrupt or Be Disrupted

Disrupt or Be Disrupted

NAVIGATING INNOVATION IN THE DIGITAL AGE

B. Vincent

QuantumQuill Press

Contents

Introduction

The Ascent of Computerized Disturbance:

Lately, the world has seen an uncommon flood of computerized interruptions clearing across ventures, reshaping conventional plans of action and rocking the boat. From retail to finance, medical services to transportation, no area has been invulnerable to the groundbreaking force of innovation. As progressions in man-made reasoning, blockchain, and the Web of Things keep on speeding up, the speed of disturbance just escalates, setting out both open doors and dangers for associations around the world.

Computerized disturbance isn't only a passing pattern; it addresses a crucial change in how organizations work and contend in the 21st century. Organizations that once appreciated strength in their particular business sectors are currently ending up on edge as nimble new companies and educated disruptors influence development to rethink industry principles and catch a piece of the pie.

At the core of this interruption lies the democratization of innovation, which has brought hindrances down to passage and engaged people and small groups to develop and upset laid-out occupants. The ascent of distributed computing, open-source programming, and worldwide networks has empowered new businesses to scale quickly and contend with industry goliaths on a level battleground.

Additionally, shopper assumptions are developing along with innovative headways, driving interest in customized encounters, on-request benefits, and consistent computerized associations. Organizations that neglect to adjust to these moving inclinations risk being abandoned, consigned to the records of history as useful examples of botched open doors.

In this period of advanced disturbance, the capacity to expect change, embrace development, and turn rapidly has become central to endurance. Associations should develop a culture of trial and error and deftness, where disappointment is seen not as a difficulty but rather as a venturing stone to progress. By outfitting the force of innovation and embracing disturbance as an open door as opposed to a danger, organizations can situate themselves for long-term development and flourishing in the computerized age.

Grasping Advancement in the Computerized Period:

Development has forever been the backbone of progress, driving cultural progress and monetary development. Notwithstanding, in the computerized age, development takes on another aspect, energized by uncommon access to information, computational power, and inter-connected frameworks. Understanding the complexities of advance-ment in this setting is fundamental for associations looking to flourish in an undeniably serious and dynamic scene.

At its center, development in the computerized age is described by nimbleness, flexibility, and a tenacious spotlight on addressing client needs. Dissimilar to customary models of development, which fre-quently followed straight and successive cycles, advanced development is iterative and nonlinear, directed by fast trial and error and consis-tent input circles. This iterative methodology permits associations to rapidly test speculations, gain from disappointments, and repeat on arrangements, speeding up the speed of advancement and decreasing the opportunity to showcase.

Also, advanced development is innately cooperative, drawing upon different viewpoints and abilities from across disciplines and ventures. Open development stages, hackathons, and cooperative biological sys-tems empower associations to take advantage of outside ability and assets, driving inventiveness and cultivating a culture of co-creation.

In the computerized period, development stretches out past items and administrations to envelop plans of action, cycles, and, surpris-ingly, whole businesses. Troublesome innovations, for example, block-chain, man-made brainpower, and the Web of Things, are improving existing contributions as well as essentially reshaping esteem chains and reclassifying the standards of rivalry.

To flourish in this climate, associations should embrace an outlook of constant learning and transformation, cultivating a culture that supports trial and error, risk-taking, and gaining from disappointment. By engaging representatives to think imaginatively, challenge suspicions, and investigate novel thoughts, associations can release the maximum capacity of their labor force and drive manageable advancement.

At last, understanding development in the computerized age requires a readiness to embrace vulnerability, explore intricacy, and embrace change as a constant. By developing a culture of advancement and putting resources into the capacities and innovations that empower it, associations can situate themselves as pioneers in their separate ventures and drive significant effect in a consistently developing world.

Why Customary Models Are Falling Flat:

Even with a quick mechanical disturbance, customary plans of action are attempting to stay pertinent in the present computerized scene. Based on standards of strength, consistency, and a progressive system, these models were intended for a period characterized by sluggish-paced change and generally stable economic situations. Be that as it may, in the computerized age, where advancement cycles are estimated in months as opposed to years and client assumptions are continually developing, customary models are progressively deficient.

One of the essential reasons conventional models are fizzling is their innate unbending nature and protection from change. Authoritative designs worked around siloed offices, and hierarchical dynamic cycles are unprepared to respond agilely to moving business sector elements or arising dangers. Thus, organizations wind up stalled by administration, incapable of benefiting from new open doors or adjusting to changing client inclinations.

Additionally, conventional models are often based on obsolete suspicions about esteem creation and upper hand. In the present computerized economy, where information is the new money and environments trump individual items or administrations, the principles of rivalry have in a general sense changed. Organizations that grip to obsolete thoughts of upper hand dependent exclusively upon item elements or brand faithfulness risk being surpassed by additional little contenders who influence information-driven bits of knowledge and environment associations to convey prevalent client encounters.

Moreover, customary models are thwarted by heritage frameworks and cycles that are delayed to adjust to new advancements or market patterns. Lumbering IT frameworks, obsolete heritage frameworks, and dug-in approaches to working can smother advancement and block spryness, making it hard for associations to turn because of changing economic situations.

Also, customary models frequently focus on momentary benefit over long-haul maintainability, driving organizations to zero in on improving existing plans of action as opposed to investigating new open doors for development. This nearsighted spotlight on effectiveness and cost-cutting can block advancement and leave organizations helpless against interruption by more ground-breaking contenders.

Considering these difficulties, associations should perceive the limits of customary models and embrace new ways to deal with the authoritative plan and the executives that are more qualified for the real factors of the computerized age. By encouraging a culture of spryness, trial and error, and ceaseless learning, organizations can situate themselves to flourish in a time characterized by disturbance and change.

The Significance of Flexibility:

In the rapidly developing business scene, flexibility has arisen as a foundation for progress for associations looking to flourish despite vulnerability and disturbance. Dissimilar to security and consistency, which were once valued characteristics in customary plans of action, versatility is the capacity to respond rapidly and successfully to evolving conditions, utilizing new open doors and moderating expected dangers.

At its center, flexibility is about something other than responding to outer powers; it's about proactively molding one's fate in a world described by consistent transition. Associations that embrace flexibility make due in violent times as well as flourish, taking advantage of chances for development and advancement that others might disregard.

One of the critical advantages of versatility is its capacity to encourage flexibility despite affliction. By keeping an adaptable mentality and a readiness to embrace change, associations can weather storms that would somehow wreck less versatile contenders. Whether confronting an unexpected change in economic situations, a troublesome new contestant, or a worldwide emergency, versatile associations are better prepared to turn rapidly and track down savvy fixes to unanticipated difficulties.

Besides, versatility empowers associations to profit by opening doors and patterns and situating themselves as pioneers in their separate enterprises. By remaining receptive to changes in client inclinations, mechanical headways, and market elements, versatile associations can distinguish new income streams, enter new business sectors, and disturb occupants before they get an opportunity to respond.

Likewise, flexibility cultivates a culture of development and consistent improvement, engaging workers at all levels to contribute their thoughts and examinations to new methodologies. Instead of gripping to obsolete approaches to working or settled processes, versatile associations embrace change as an impetus for development, empowering representatives to rock the boat and push the limits of what's conceivable.

At last, versatility isn't simply a positive quality for associations; it's an endurance basic in a time characterized by disturbance and change. By focusing on versatility and developing a culture that values adaptability, spryness, and flexibility, associations can situate themselves for long-term progress in an uncertain and steadily impacting world.

Outline of the Book's Construction:

In "Upset or Be Disturbed: Exploring Development in the Computerized Age," we set out on an excursion to investigate the elements of disturbance and development in the present quickly advancing business scene. This book is organized to give perusers a far-reaching comprehension of the powers driving computerized interruption and furnish them with functional procedures for exploring the difficulties and open doors it presents.

In the accompanying parts, we will dig into different parts of disturbance and advancement, covering subjects like the essentials of interruption, systems for driving development, exploring administrative difficulties, building strength, and investigating future patterns and arising advancements. Every part is intended to offer noteworthy bits of knowledge and genuine guides to assist perusers with applying these ideas to their own associations.

Part 1 sets the stage by inspecting the ascent of computerized interruption and the variables driving it, giving perusers a basic comprehension of the difficulties and open doors introduced by the computerized age. We investigate why conventional models are coming up short and why versatility has become more basic than any time in recent memory in the present quick-moving business climate.

Part 2 dives into the basics of disturbance, characterizing what disturbance implies in the advanced age and investigating the attributes of problematic innovations. Through contextual investigations and models, we show how associations can recognize and answer problematic dangers and take advantage of chances for development.

In Section 3, we set out on the computerized change venture, directing perusers through the most common way of surveying their present status, defining change objectives, and building a culture of development inside their associations. We investigate the job of arising advances in driving computerized change and give pragmatic techniques for defeating protection from change.

Section 4 spotlights methodologies for driving troublesome advancement, covering themes such as the dexterous turn of events, open development, plan thinking, information-driven independent direction, and trial and error. Through genuine models and noteworthy bits of knowledge, we show the way that associations can encourage a culture of development and drive significant change.

In Part 5, we investigate the administrative difficulties related to computerized disturbance, giving perusers techniques for drawing in with controllers, building moral and dependable advancements, and upholding administrative change. We additionally look at the moral contemplations inborn in advancement and talk about the significance of moral authority in the computerized age.

All through the book, perusers will experience contextual analyses, models, and useful activities intended to build up key ideas and assist perusers with applying them to their own associations. Toward the end of this excursion, perusers will have acquired a more profound comprehension of the powers driving computerized disturbance and the systems expected to explore them effectively in the computerized age.

1

Chapter 1: Understanding Disruption

The Ascent of Computerized Disturbance:

Lately, the scene of worldwide business has been permanently modified by the inescapable power of computerized interruption. What used to be consistent, laid-out businesses presently end up in the midst of a hurricane of progress, driven by the tireless headway of innovation. From retail to back, medical care to transportation, basically no area has been left immaculate by this computerized upheaval.

The quintessence of this disturbance lies in the extraordinary force of innovation, which has not just reclassified the manner in which we collaborate with the world but has likewise, on a very basic level, modified the standards of commitment for organizations. Never again can organizations depend entirely on conventional strategies to keep up with their portion of the overall industry; all things considered, they should adjust to the always-moving tides of development or hazards being cleared away by additional spry contenders.

This ascent of computerized disturbance isn't just a passing pattern; it addresses a seismic change in the actual texture of our economy. It is a demonstration of the democratization of innovation, which has engaged people and small groups to rock the boat and upset whole businesses. From the ascent of new businesses to the expansion of open-source programming, the hindrances to section have never been lower, taking into consideration exceptional degrees of rivalry and development.

Besides, computerized interruption isn't bound to the domain of innovation; a social peculiarity contacts each part of our lives. Customer assumptions are developing dangerously fast, determined by a craving for customized encounters, on-request benefits, and consistent computerized cooperation. Organizations that neglect to adjust to these moving inclinations risk becoming relics of the past, transferred to the chronicles of history as useful examples of botched open doors.

In this period of computerized disturbance, the capacity to expect change, embrace advancement, and turn rapidly has become vital for endurance. Organizations should develop a culture of trial and error and spryness where disappointment isn't just acknowledged but celebrated as an essential step on the way to progress. By tackling the force of innovation and embracing disturbance as an open door as opposed to a danger, organizations can situate themselves for long-term development and thrive in the computerized age.

Why Customary Models Are Falling Flat:

Amidst the computerized upheaval, conventional plans of action are ending up progressively in conflict with the quickly developing scene. Based upon standards of soundness, consistency, and order, these models were intended for a period described by sluggish-paced change and moderately stable economic situations. Notwithstanding, in the present hyperconnected world, where development cycles are estimated in months as opposed to years and client assumptions are continually moving, customary models are battling to keep pace.

One of the essential reasons customary models are vacillating is their intrinsic unbending nature and protection from change. Hierarchical designs worked around siloed divisions, and hierarchical dynamic cycles are mismatched to answer rapidly to the powerful idea of the present business climate. Subsequently, organizations end up stalled by administration, unfit to gain new open doors or adjust to arising dangers.

Also, customary models are often based on obsolete suppositions about esteem creation and upper hand. In the computerized economy, where information is the new money and environments trump individual items or administrations, the principles of rivalry have in a general sense changed. Organizations that stick to obsolete thoughts of upper hand dependent exclusively upon item highlights or brand dedication risk being overwhelmed by additional deft contenders who influence information-driven bits of knowledge and environment associations to convey prevalent client encounters.

Besides, customary models are impeded by inheritance frameworks and cycles that are delayed to adjust to new advances or market patterns. Unwieldy IT foundations, obsolete heritage frameworks, and settled approaches to working can smother development and obstruct deftness, making it hard for associations to turn in light of changing economic situations.

Likewise, conventional models frequently focus on transient benefit over long-haul manageability, driving organizations to zero in on upgrading existing plans of action as opposed to investigating new open doors for development. This nearsighted spotlight on productivity and cost-cutting can ruin advancement and leave organizations defenseless against interruption by more ground-breaking contenders.

Considering these difficulties, associations should perceive the impediments of customary models and embrace new ways to deal with authoritative plans and boards that are more qualified for the real factors of the computerized age. By cultivating a culture of deftness, trial and error, and consistent learning, organizations can situate themselves to flourish in a period characterized by disturbance and change.

Recognizing Problematic Dangers:

In the consistently changing scene of business, the capacity to expect and answer problematic dangers is paramount for associations trying to stay serious. Disturbance can come in many forms, from mechanical developments that reclassify industry norms to shifts in customer conduct that overturn conventional plans of action. Perceiving and understanding these dangers is the most important move toward actually tending to them and jumping all over chances for development.

To distinguish troublesome dangers, associations should embrace a proactive way to deal with observing the outside climate and examining for arising patterns. This includes keeping up to date with improvements in innovation, guidelines, and purchaser inclinations, as well as watching out for the activities of contenders and potential disruptors. By leading standard statistical surveying, drawing in with industry specialists, and partaking in industry discussions and meetings, associations can acquire significant bits of knowledge about potential disruptors not too far off.

Notwithstanding outer variables, associations should likewise survey their own interior capacities and weaknesses. This includes assessing the strength of their current plans of action, the adaptability of their authoritative designs, and the profundity of their ability pool. By leading interior appraisals and recognizing regions for development, associations can all the more likely position themselves to answer problematic dangers and gain by arising potential open doors.

When problematic dangers have been distinguished, associations should foster procedures for tending to them successfully. This might include putting resources into new advancements, investigating associations with new businesses or other creative organizations, or rethinking existing items or administrations to more readily meet developing client needs. By adopting a proactive approach to disturbance, associations can transform likely dangers into potential open doors for development and advancement, situating themselves as pioneers in their separate enterprises.

Embracing Disturbance as an Open Door:

While interruption may at first be seen as a danger, wise associations remember it as a chance for development. In the present speedy business climate, where change is consistent and contest is furious, embracing disturbance isn't just important for endurance but additionally fundamental for long-haul achievement.

The most important phase in embracing disturbance as an open door is to develop an outlook of flexibility and strength within the association. This includes cultivating a culture that supports trial and error, risk-taking, and consistent realizing, where disappointment is seen not as a misfortune but rather as a significant opportunity for growth. By enabling representatives to think imaginatively, rock the boat, and investigate groundbreaking thoughts, associations can open up the maximum capacity of their labor force and drive significant development.

Besides, embracing interruption expects associations to take on a proactive way to deal with change instead of essentially responding to outside powers. This implies effectively searching out open doors for disturbance, whether through the reception of new innovations, the investigation of new business sectors, or the production of new plans of action. By remaining on the ball and expecting future patterns, associations can situate themselves as pioneers in their particular enterprises and gain an upper hand over their companions.

Also, embracing interruption expects associations to upset themselves. This might include tearing up existing items or administrations, stripping from heritage business lines, or rethinking the manner in which they carry on with work by and large. While this might be awkward temporarily, remaining applicable and cutthroat in a consistently changing marketplace is often fundamental.

Eventually, embracing interruption as an open door requires a readiness to embrace vulnerability, proceed with reasonable courses of action, and rock the boat. By encouraging a culture of development and flexibility, associations can make due in a problematic climate as well as flourish, situating themselves for long-term outcomes in the computerized age.

2

Chapter 2: The Digital Transformation

Attributes of Troublesome Innovations:

In the always-advancing scene of development, certain advancements stand apart for their troublesome potential, reshaping businesses and testing laid-out standards. Understanding the critical qualities of these problematic advancements is fundamental for associations trying to explore the computerized change and gain by arising potential open doors.

At the core of problematic advances lies their capacity to rock the boat and overturn customary plans of action. Not at all like gradual advancements that enhance existing items or cycles, problematic innovations present totally better approaches for getting things done, frequently delivering past arrangements that are outdated.

One of the main traits of troublesome advancements is their capacity to democratize access to previously selected assets or abilities. Whether it's the democratization of data through the web, the democratization of creation through 3D printing, or the democratization of money through blockchain, these innovations engage people and little associations to rival laid-out occupants on a level battleground.

Besides, troublesome innovations frequently show remarkable

development bends, quickly gaining momentum and versatility once they arrive at a basic tipping point. This remarkable development is energized by network impacts, where the worth of an innovation increases as additional clients take on it, creating an idealistic pattern of reception and extension.

One more quality of troublesome innovations is their capability to empower new plans of action and income streams. Whether it's the membership-based plan of action empowered by distributed computing, the sharing economy worked with by distributed stages, or the decentralized money environment empowered by blockchain, troublesome advances open up additional opportunities for development and worth creation.

Moreover, troublesome innovations are often portrayed by their capacity to obscure the limits between businesses, opening new doors for joint effort and contest. As limits disintegrate and ventures merge, associations should be ready to adjust to new environments and organizations, utilizing their assets to explore the moving scene of advancement.

In summary, understanding the qualities of troublesome advancements is fundamental for associations trying to flourish in the computerized age. By embracing these advances and the open doors they present, associations can situate themselves for outcome in a steadily changing and progressively serious commercial center.

Contextual investigations of fruitful disruptors:

In the chronicles of business history, there are various instances of organizations that have ascended to conspicuousness by utilizing troublesome advances to challenge occupants and reshape whole enterprises. These contextual analyses act as important wellsprings of knowledge for associations trying to explore the computerized change and benefit from arising valuable open doors.

One such contextual investigation is that of Airbnb, an organization that reformed the cordiality business by bridling the force of the sharing economy and distributed networks. By empowering people to lease their extra rooms or properties to voyagers, Airbnb disturbed the customary inn industry, offering explorers a more reasonable and customized option in contrast to conventional facilities.

Another model is that of Netflix, which disturbed media outlets by progressing from a DVD rental to a streaming stage, profiting from headways in broadband innovation and changing purchaser inclinations. By offering a huge library of on-demand content satisfied for a portion of the expense of link memberships, Netflix changed the manner in which individuals consume media, forcing conventional players to adjust or confront oldness.

Likewise, Uber upset the transportation business by presenting a ride-hailing stage that interfaces travelers with drivers through a portable application. By utilizing GPS innovation and the omnipresence of cell phones, Uber disrupts metropolitan transportation, offering travelers a more helpful and practical option in contrast to customary cabs.

These contextual investigations feature the extraordinary force of troublesome advancements and the potential open doors they present for associations ready to embrace development and rock the boat. By concentrating on the procedures and approaches of fruitful disruptors, associations can acquire important insights into how to distinguish and gain by opening doors in their own businesses.

In addition, these contextual analyses likewise highlight the significance of spryness and versatility despite disturbance. For each situation, fruitful disruptors had the option to turn rapidly in light of changing business sector elements, utilizing their assets to gain by arising patterns and outsmart competitors.

All in all, situational investigations of effective disruptors offer important illustrations for associations looking to flourish in the advanced age. By concentrating on the methodologies and approaches of these pioneers, associations can acquire the bits of knowledge and motivation expected to explore the intricacies of disturbance and arise as pioneers in their separate enterprises.

Recognizing Possible Disturbance in Your Industry:

In the high-speed universe of business, the capacity to expect and answer troublesome dangers is significant for associations trying to keep up with their strategic advantage. While disturbance can sometimes show up as an unanticipated occasion, there are in many cases early admonition signs that associations can pay special attention to distinguish possible interruptions in their industry before they become completely manifest.

One critical mark of potential interruption is the development of new advances or plans of action that can possibly, on a very basic level, reshape the cutthroat scene. Whether it's the approach of blockchain innovation in finance, the ascent of web-based business in retail, or the multiplication of on-request benefits in transportation, new innovations can frequently act as harbingers of disturbance, flagging a change in client inclinations or market elements.

One more sign of potential disturbance is changes in shopper conduct or inclinations. As shopper assumptions develop in light of mechanical progressions, segment shifts, or social changes, associations should be sensitive to these movements and adjust their methodologies in a similar manner. Whether it's the developing inclination for supportability and moral utilization or the rising interest in customized encounters and on-request benefits, changes in shopper conduct can frequently anticipate disturbance in customary enterprises.

Moreover, associations ought to be careful for indications of market immersion or stagnation, which can create ready circumstances for interruption. Whether it's declining overall revenues, easing back development rates, or expanding competition from new participants, these markers can flag that conventional plans of action are arriving at their cutoff points and are ready for interruption by additional inventive and lithe contenders.

Also, associations ought to be aware of administrative changes or international improvements that could influence their industry. Whether new guidelines, even the odds for novices, or international pressures that upset worldwide inventory chains, these outside elements can frequently act as impetuses for interruption, setting out the two difficulties and opening doors for associations that are ready to adjust.

By staying watchful and proactive in observing these early admonition signs, associations can situate themselves to recognize and answer expected disturbances before they become completely manifest. Whether through putting resources into new advances, investigating new plans of action, or fashioning vital associations, associations that can expect and adjust to disturbance will be better prepared to flourish in a steadily changing and progressively serious commercial center.

Embracing Interruption as an Open Door:

In the domain of business, disturbance is frequently seen with dread, seen as a danger to laid-out standards and practices. Notwithstanding, canny associations perceive that disturbance likewise presents a remarkable chance for development and reevaluation. By embracing disturbance as an open door as opposed to a danger, associations can situate themselves to flourish in a consistently changing and progressively cutthroat commercial center.

One of the critical advantages of embracing interruption is the potential for advancement and change. Interruption powers associations to think innovatively, rock the boat, and investigate better approaches for getting things done. Whether it's utilizing new advancements to smooth out tasks, taking advantage of developing business sectors to extend client reach, or reconsidering plans of action to all the more likely meet advancing client needs, interruption catalyzes development and drives significant change.

Besides, embracing disturbance permits associations to remain on the ball and keep an upper hand in the commercial center. By proactively expecting and answering troublesome dangers, associations can situate themselves as pioneers in their separate ventures, acquiring first-mover benefits and forming the fate of their business sectors.

Moreover, disturbance gives associations a potential chance to separate themselves from contenders and cut out an exceptional incentive. Whether it's through offering creative items or administrations, conveying excellent client encounters, or spearheading new plans of action, associations that embrace disturbance can separate themselves in the commercial center and assemble enduring upper hands.

Furthermore, embracing disturbance encourages a culture of nimbleness, versatility, and strength within associations. By empowering workers to embrace change, proceed with carefully weighed-out courses of action, and gain from disappointment, associations can construct groups that are better prepared to explore the vulnerabilities of the advanced age and flourish in unique and quickly developing conditions.

All in all, embracing disturbance as an open door is fundamental for associations trying to flourish in the computerized age. By cultivating a culture of development, dexterity, and flexibility, associations can situate themselves to profit by arising potential open doors, separating themselves from contenders, and keeping an upper hand in a consistently changing and progressively cutthroat commercial center.

Chapter 3: Navigating the Innovation Landscape

Evaluating your present status:

Prior to leaving on any excursion of advancement and computerized change, it is fundamental for associations to assess their present status. This includes a careful evaluation of the association's capacity, culture, and status for change. By understanding where they stand today, associations can all the more likely distinguish regions for development and outline a course toward a more inventive future.

The evaluation interaction starts with a complete examination of the association's current capacities and assets. This includes assessing the abilities and skills of representatives, the strength of the association's innovation framework, and the adequacy of its current cycles and frameworks. By distinguishing solid areas and shortcomings, associations can figure out where to concentrate their endeavors and speculations to drive significant change.

As well as assessing capacities, associations should likewise survey their hierarchical culture and availability for advancement. This includes looking at elements such as initiative, capacity to bear hazards and disappointment, and receptiveness to novel thoughts and approaches to working. By understanding the social hindrances that might obstruct development, associations can foster systems to defeat opposition and cultivate a culture that supports trial and error and inventiveness.

Besides, associations should survey the outer elements that might influence their capacity to successfully advance. This incorporates breaking down market elements, serious tensions, administrative imperatives, and arising patterns in innovation and buyer conduct. By remaining sensitive to these outside powers, associations can all the more likely expect difficulties and potential open doors and change their development methodologies appropriately.

At long last, the evaluation cycle ought to likewise include drawing in with partners at all levels of the association to acquire bits of knowledge about their points of view, concerns, and goals for what's to come. By requesting input from workers, clients, accomplices, and other key partners, associations can guarantee that their advancement endeavors are aligned with the requirements and assumptions of those they serve.

In outline, surveying the association's present status is a basic initial phase in exploring the development scene. By checking out their capacities, culture, and outer climate, associations can lay the foundation for effective development and computerized change drives, situating themselves for long-term progress in a quickly developing commercial center.

Building a Culture of Development:

Development isn't just about embracing new innovations or executing clever thoughts; likewise, cultivating a culture values innovativeness, trial and error, and nonstop learning. Building such a culture is fundamental for associations looking to flourish in the rapidly changing business climate, where the capacity to adjust and develop is vital for progress.

At the core of a culture of development lies a mentality that energizes interest and embraces risk-taking. Workers ought to feel engaged to scrutinize business as usual, challenge customary reasoning, and investigate additional opportunities unafraid of disappointment. By cultivating a culture that praises trial and error and learning from mistakes, associations can release the imaginative capability of their labor force and drive significant development.

Besides, building a culture of development requires initiative, help, and responsibility from the top administration. Pioneers should establish the vibe by supporting development as an essential need and showing others how it is done through their activities and ways of behaving. This includes dispensing assets and financing for advancement drives, giving open doors to workers to foster new abilities and capacities, and perceiving and remunerating creative commitments.

Notwithstanding initiative, fabricating a culture of development likewise requires establishing a climate that encourages cooperation and cross-fertilization of thoughts. This includes separating storehouses and empowering correspondence and cooperation across divisions and groups. By uniting assorted viewpoints and aptitudes, associations can produce new experiences and ways to deal with critical thinking, driving advancement and innovation.

Besides, building a culture of development includes furnishing workers with the instruments, assets, and backing they need to really enhance. This might include financial planning for preparation and advancement programs, giving admittance to development labs or creator spaces, or executing cycles and instruments to help with thought and trial and error. By outfitting representatives with vital abilities and assets, associations can enable them to develop and drive positive change within the association.

In summary, fostering a culture of development is fundamental for associations looking to flourish in the present speedy and serious business climate. By cultivating a culture that values innovativeness, trial and error, and nonstop learning, associations can release the maximum capacity of their labor force and drive significant development that drives reasonable development and the upper hand.

Utilizing Arising Advancements:

Advancement frequently remains inseparable from the reception and reconciliation of arising innovations that can possibly change ventures and upset business processes. Associations that can recognize and use these advancements successfully can acquire an upper hand and position themselves as pioneers in their separate fields. Thusly, it is pivotal for associations to remain informed about the most recent headways and patterns in innovation and investigate how they can be applied to drive advancement and create esteem.

One vital part of utilizing arising advancements is understanding the particular requirements and difficulties confronting the association and distinguishing innovations that can actually address them. Whether it's man-made reasoning, blockchain, the Web of Things, or increased reality, every innovation offers extraordinary capacities and possible applications. By directing an exhaustive evaluation of the association's targets and necessities, pioneers can recognize innovations that are most ideal to their requirements and create a guide for their execution.

In addition, associations should likewise consider the more extensive biological system of advances and how they cooperate with each other. For instance, the mix of man-made reasoning and huge information examination can open strong experiences and empower associations to pursue information-driven choices progressively. Also, the combination of blockchain innovation with inventory network frameworks can improve straightforwardness, discernibility, and trust across the value chain. By understanding how these innovations supplement each other, associations can foster coordinated arrangements that convey more noteworthy worth and effect.

Moreover, associations should likewise consider the possible dangers and difficulties related to the reception of arising advances. These may incorporate worries around information protection and security, administrative consistency, moral contemplations, and the effect on existing business cycles and work processes. By proactively tending to these difficulties and executing powerful gamble-the-board systems, associations can moderate possible dangers and guarantee smooth progress toward new innovations.

As well as tending to chances, associations should likewise put resources into the important foundation, ability, and capacities to help the reception and joining of arising advancements. This might include recruiting or upskilling workers with ability in regions like information science, online protection, and programming advancement, as well as putting resources into the essential equipment, programming, and IT foundation to help new advancements.

In outline, utilizing arising advancements is fundamental for associations looking to drive development and keep an upper hand in the present computerized age. By remaining informed about the most recent progressions, understanding the particular requirements and difficulties confronting the association, and proactively tending to dangers and difficulties, associations can bridle the extraordinary force of innovation to drive significant change and make an incentive for their clients and partners.

Beating Protection from Change:

While development and advanced change are fundamental for remaining cutthroat in the present quick-moving business climate, they frequently face obstruction from inside the association. Representatives might be reluctant to embrace change because of dread of the unknown, worries about employer stability, or hesitance to get out of their usual ranges of familiarity. Defeating this obstruction requires coordinated work to address the underlying drivers of opposition and establish a climate that cultivates transparency, cooperation, and a common sense of direction.

One of the best ways to protect against change is by encouraging clear and straightforward correspondence throughout the association. Pioneers should explain the explanations for the requirement for change, impart the advantages and valuable open doors it presents, and address any worries or confusions that might emerge. By giving representatives a reasonable comprehension of the reasoning behind change and including them in the dynamic cycle, associations can encourage a feeling of responsibility and purchase, making them more open to change.

Additionally, associations should give representatives the vital help and assets they need to successfully explore the change. This might include financial planning for preparing and advancement projects to fabricate the abilities and capacities expected for outcome in the computerized age, giving access to training and coaching to assist workers with exploring the difficulties of progress, and setting out open doors for coordinated effort and information sharing to cultivate a culture of constant learning and improvement.

As well as offering help, associations should likewise address any primary or social obstructions that might thwart advancement and change. This might include separating storehouses and advancing cross-practical joint effort, enabling representatives to face challenges and analysis with novel thoughts, and fulfilling and perceiving imaginative commitments. By establishing a climate that values inventiveness, trial and error, and variety of thought, associations can beat protection from change and cultivate a culture of development and dexterity.

Moreover, associations should show others how it is done by exhibiting a pledge to change at all levels of the association. Pioneers should display the ways of behaving and mentalities they wish to find in others, showing receptiveness to groundbreaking thoughts, readiness to face challenges, and strength notwithstanding affliction. By showing others how it is done and supporting change starting from the top, pioneers can rouse certainty and confidence in the association's vision and bearing, making it simpler for workers to embrace change and drive development.

In outline, defeating protection from change is fundamental for associations trying to drive development and advanced change. By encouraging clear and straightforward correspondence, offering help and assets, tending to underlying and social obstructions, and showing others how it is done, associations can establish a climate that is helpful for change and development, situating themselves for long-term progress in a quickly developing business scene.

4

Chapter 4: The Role of Leadership in Driving Innovation

Cultivating a Culture of Development:

At the core of any effective development drive lies a culture that cultivates innovativeness, trial and error, and an eagerness to rock the boat. As the essential draftsmen of hierarchical culture, pioneers assume a crucial role in forming the climate in which development flourishes. By establishing the vibe and laying out assumptions for conduct and perspectives towards development, pioneers can create a culture that values and prizes advancement at all levels of the association.

One of the vital obligations of authority in encouraging a culture of development is to support the significance of development and impart its essential importance to the association. Pioneers should explain a convincing vision for development, featuring its part in driving development, encouraging seriousness, and conveying worth to clients and partners. By adjusting development endeavors to the association's essential goals, pioneers can guarantee that advancement turns into a central piece of the hierarchical DNA.

Also, pioneers should establish a climate that empowers and supports trial and error and risk-taking. This includes eliminating hindrances to development, like organization, order, and apprehension about disappointment, and enabling representatives to investigate groundbreaking thoughts and approaches. Pioneers should make mental security inside the association, where representatives feel open to going ahead with potentially dangerous courses of action and gaining from their slip-ups unafraid of retaliation.

Moreover, pioneers should put resources into the advancement of abilities and capacities that are fundamental for development. This might include giving preparation and advancement projects to construct imaginative reasoning, critical thinking, and joint effort abilities, as well as encouraging a culture of persistent learning and improvement. By putting resources into the improvement of representatives, pioneers can guarantee that the association has the ability and mastery expected to drive significant development.

As well as encouraging a culture of development inside, pioneers should likewise develop outside organizations and associations that can work with advancement. This might include teaming up with clients, providers, the scholarly world, and other outside partners to co-make arrangements, share information and best practices, and access new business sectors and potential open doors. By utilizing outside organizations, pioneers can take advantage of a more extensive environment of thoughts and mastery, driving development and making an incentive for the association.

In summary, encouraging a culture of development is fundamental for associations looking to flourish in the present high-speed and cut-throat business climate. By advocating the significance of advancement, establishing a climate that upholds trial and error and chance-taking, putting resources into the improvement of abilities and capacities, and developing outside organizations and associations, pioneers can establish a climate where development thrives, driving development and accomplishment for the association.

Engaging Workers to Advance:

The position of authority in driving development stretches beyond establishing the vibe and cultivating a culture of imagination; it likewise includes enabling workers at all levels of the association to contribute their thoughts and bits of knowledge to the development cycle. Perceiving that development can emerge from anybody, no matter what their situation or foundation, pioneers should establish a climate where each worker feels engaged and urged to advance.

One way pioneers can engage workers to advance is by furnishing them with the independence and adaptability to investigate groundbreaking thoughts and trial various methodologies. This includes giving representatives the opportunity to take responsibility for work, settle on choices independently, and seek after projects that line up with their inclinations and assets. By confiding in representatives to step up to the plate and enhance freely, pioneers can take advantage of the maximum capacity of their labor force and open new wellsprings of imagination and advancement.

Besides, pioneers should give workers the assets and backing they need to actually improve. This might incorporate giving admittance to preparation and advancement projects to fabricate abilities and capacities applicable to development, dispensing devoted time and financing for advancement projects, and making stations for workers to team up and share thoughts. By putting resources into the improvement of representatives and furnishing them with the essential assets and backing, pioneers can enable them to face challenges and investigate additional opportunities, driving significant development inside the association.

Besides, pioneers should create a culture that values and prizes development, perceiving and praising the commitments of representatives who exceed everyone's expectations to drive development. This might include carrying out proper acknowledgment programs, for example, development grants or representative bright lights, as well as setting out casual open doors for workers to impart their victories and learnings to their companions. By commending development and perceiving the accomplishments of workers, pioneers can support a culture that energizes and remunerates innovativeness and drive.

As well as engaging individual representatives, pioneers should likewise encourage cooperation and collaboration across the association to drive aggregate advancement. This includes separating storehouses and setting out open doors for cross-utilitarian coordinated effort, where workers from various divisions and foundations can meet up to share thoughts, team up on undertakings, and influence their different viewpoints and mastery to drive development. By cultivating a culture of coordinated effort and collaboration, pioneers can outfit the aggregate insight of the association and drive development at scale.

In outline, enabling representatives to enhance is fundamental for associations looking to drive significant change and remain serious in the present unique business climate. By furnishing representatives with the independence, assets, and backing they need to really improve, creating a culture that values and rewards development, and encouraging joint effort and collaboration across the association, pioneers can open up the maximum capacity of their labor force and drive development that conveys worth and drives accomplishment for the association.

Setting a Dream for Development:

An unmistakable and convincing vision is fundamental for directing development drives and adjusting endeavors across the association. Pioneers assume a basic role in setting this vision, articulating a reasonable course for development that rouses and persuades representatives to embrace change and seek out new open doors. By setting an intense and aggressive vision for development, pioneers can create a sense of direction and bearing that guides navigation and drives progress towards hierarchical objectives.

One of the vital obligations of administration in setting a dream for development is to characterize the ideal results and goals of advancement drives. This includes recognizing the essential needs and areas of the center where development can greatly affect the association's prosperity. Whether it's further developing client encounters, driving functional proficiency, or cultivating item development, pioneers should verbalize clear and explicit objectives that give a guide to development endeavors.

Besides, pioneers should impart the vision for advancement to actually guarantee arrangement and purchase across the association. This includes connecting with representatives at all levels, sharing the reasoning behind the vision, and featuring the advantages and amazing open doors it presents. By imparting the vision in a convincing and powerful way, pioneers can motivate excitement and responsibility among representatives, revitalizing them around a typical reason and lighting their energy for development.

Moreover, pioneers should show others how it is done and exhibit their obligation to the vision for development through their activities and ways of behaving. This might include effectively partaking in advancement drives, giving assets and backing to development endeavors, and commending and perceiving imaginative accomplishments. By exhibiting their obligation to development, pioneers can cultivate a culture that values and focuses on advancement, empowering representatives to embrace change and seek out groundbreaking thoughts and valuable open doors.

As well as setting the vision for development, pioneers should likewise make instruments for estimating progress and assessing the effect of advancement drives. This includes laying out key execution pointers (KPIs) and measurements to follow the progress of advancement endeavors and guarantee arrangements with authoritative targets. By checking progress against these measurements and pursuing information-driven choices, pioneers can distinguish regions for development and change their advancement methodologies likewise, guaranteeing that advancement endeavors are conveying substantial outcomes and driving significant change inside the association.

In summary, setting a vision for development is fundamental for directing and adjusting endeavors across the association. By characterizing clear goals, conveying the vision really, showing others how it was done, and laying out instruments for estimating progress, pioneers can make a guide for development that moves and propels workers to embrace change, seek after new open doors, and drive accomplishment for the association.

Apportioning Assets for Development:

Advancement requires something beyond thoughts; it additionally requires assets—whether monetary, human, or time-related—to carry those plans to completion. Pioneers assume an essential role in designating assets to really help development drives and guarantee their prosperity. By focusing on and dispensing assets decisively, pioneers can augment the effect of advancement endeavors and drive practical development and seriousness for the association.

One of the vital obligations of authority in distributing assets for advancement is to focus on ventures in light of their capability to convey worth and drive hierarchical goals. This includes assessing the return on capital invested in various advancement drives, gauging the likely advantages against the expenses and dangers implied, and allotting assets to those drives that offer the best potential for progress. By zeroing in assets on high-need projects with clear essential arrangements, pioneers can guarantee that advancement endeavors are coordinated towards accomplishing substantial results that add to hierarchical achievement.

In addition, pioneers should provide sufficient financing and monetary help to fuel advancement drives and empower them to flourish. This might include designating devoted financial plans or subsidizing pools for advancement projects, giving seed subsidizing to beginning phase drives, and getting financing from outer sources, for example, investment or government awards. By putting resources into development, pioneers can establish a climate that energizes trial and error and chance-taking, driving advancement development and conveying a long-term incentive for the association.

Besides, pioneers should distribute HR to really help advancement endeavors and guarantee that the association has the ability and skill expected to drive development. This might include recruiting or up-skilling representatives with particular abilities and capacities applicable to advancement, for example, information science, plan thinking, or dexterous approaches, and making cross-useful groups to team up on development projects. By putting resources into the improvement of ability and building a different and comprehensive labor force, pioneers can develop a climate that encourages inventiveness, joint effort, and development at all levels of the association.

Notwithstanding monetary and HR considerations, pioneers should likewise allocate time and thoughtfulness regarding development drives to guarantee their prosperity. This might include making it a devoted reality for representatives to zero in on development projects, laying out advancement labs or hatcheries to help with trial and error and prototyping, and giving administration backing and direction to assist with exploring the intricacies of the advancement cycle. By focusing on development, pioneers can establish a climate where advancement flourishes and drives supportable development and intensity for the association.

In synopsis, allotting assets for advancement is fundamental for associations trying to drive significant change and remain cutthroat in the present powerful business climate. By focusing on speculations, giving subsidizing and monetary help, apportioning HR really, and putting time and consideration into development drives, pioneers can establish a climate that cultivates imagination, joint effort, and advancement, driving long-term achievement and flourishing for the association.

Showing others how it's done:

Initiative isn't just about setting a dream and distributing assets; it's likewise about showing others how it's done and exhibiting a promise to development through activities and ways of behaving. Pioneers act as good examples until the end of the association, and their perspectives and activities towards development can significantly affect worker commitment, inspiration, and readiness to embrace change.

One of the best ways for pioneers to exhibit their obligation to advancement is by effectively participating in development drives and showing others how it is done. This might include getting straightforwardly associated with advancement projects, giving involved direction and backing to project groups, and effectively contributing thoughts and experiences to the development cycle. By showing their own obligation to advancement, pioneers can motivate certainty and energy among workers, empowering them to follow suit accordingly and take responsibility for endeavors within their own areas of obligation.

Besides, pioneers should establish a climate that energizes and remunerates advancement, perceiving and commending the commitments of representatives who exceed everyone's expectations to drive development. This might include freely recognizing and lauding imaginative accomplishments, giving open doors to representatives to exhibit their work and offer accepted procedures with their friends, and integrating development into execution assessments and award frameworks. By building up a culture that values and prizes development, pioneers can create a righteous pattern of imagination and accomplishment that drives persistent improvement and development throughout the association.

Moreover, pioneers should exhibit flexibility and steadiness even with difficulties and mishaps, showing representatives that advancement is generally difficult yet merits chasing after regardless. This might include recognizing and learning from disappointment, adjusting methodologies and approaches in light of examples learned, and keeping a positive and hopeful disposition even despite difficulty. By showing versatility and determination, pioneers can rouse certainty and confidence in the association's capacity to conquer snags and accomplish its development objectives, cultivating a culture of flexibility and advancement that drives long-haul achievement.

As well as showing others how it is done inside, pioneers should likewise act as envoys for development remotely, elevating the association's obligation to advancement and cultivating associations with outside partners, like clients, accomplices, and financial backers. This might include talking at industry occasions, partaking in thought authority exercises, and drawing in with the more extensive advancement of the biological system to share bits of knowledge and best practices, trade thoughts, and investigate potential cooperation. By supporting development remotely, pioneers can improve the association's standing as a forerunner in advancement and draw in new abilities, clients, and potential open doors that drive development and achievement.

In outline, showing others how it is done is fundamental for pioneers trying to drive development and create a culture of constant improvement and development within their associations. By effectively partaking in development drives, establishing a climate that values and prizes development, exhibiting strength and steadiness, and filling in as representatives for advancement remotely, pioneers can rouse certainty and trust, cultivate a culture of advancement, and drive long-term achievement and success for the association.

5

Chapter 5: Building a Disruptive Business Model

Understanding Problematic Plans of Action:

In the steadily developing scene of business, the idea of troublesome advancement has become inseparable from extraordinary change and commotion. At its center, a troublesome plan of action addresses a takeoff from conventional ways to deal with esteem creation, testing laid-out standards, and reshaping whole enterprises all the while. Understanding the pith of troublesome plans of action requires a nuanced investigation of their main qualities and the manners by which they separate from customary models.

A troublesome plan of action is described by its capacity to, in a general sense, modify the cutthroat elements of an industry, frequently by focusing on underserved or neglected market fragments with creative arrangements that offer prevalent worth. Not at all like customary plans of action, which normally center around gradual upgrades to existing items or administrations, troublesome models try to make altogether new business sectors or reclassify existing ones through revolutionary development and separation.

To understand the idea of problematic plans of action completely, it's fundamental to look at certifiable models that outline their effect on occupant players and market elements. Exemplary models incorporate organizations like Uber and Airbnb, which changed transportation and friendliness enterprises separately by utilizing innovation to associate purchasers with underutilized assets in ways that were beforehand unbelievable. These disruptors didn't simply contend inside existing business sectors; they made altogether new ones, driving occupants to adjust or take a chance with outdated nature.

Besides, understanding troublesome plans of action requires perceiving that interruption is certainly not a one-time occasion but rather a continuous interaction energized by consistent development and transformation. As business sectors develop and purchaser inclinations shift, troublesome models should advance too, continually rocking the boat and pushing the limits of what's conceivable. This iterative way to deal with development empowers disruptors to remain on the ball and keep up with their strategic advantage over the long haul.

In summary, understanding troublesome plans of action is fundamental for associations trying to explore the intricacies of the advanced business scene effectively. By perceiving the central traits of problematic models, concentrating on certifiable instances of disturbance in real life, and embracing a mentality of constant development and variation, associations can situate themselves to flourish in a time characterized by quick change and vulnerability.

Distinguishing Open Doors for Interruption:

Distinguishing open doors for disturbance is a basic initial phase in building a problematic plan of action that can rock the boat and drive significant change inside an industry. This interaction includes not just perceiving existing trouble spots and shortcomings inside the market but additionally expecting future patterns and arising needs that might open doors for advancement.

One technique for distinguishing valuable open doors for interruption is to conduct a careful examination of the current market scene, inspecting variables, for example, client needs, contender contributions, and industry elements. By understanding the holes and deficiencies in the ongoing business sector, associations can recognize regions ready for disturbance and foster arrangements that address neglected needs or trouble spots more effectively than existing options.

Moreover, associations can use methods, for example, plan thinking and client venture planning, to acquire bits of knowledge about the encounters and problem areas of target clients. By feeling for clients and understanding their hidden requirements and inspirations, associations can uncover chances to advance and gain esteem in manners that resonate with their interest group.

Besides, associations can look past the prompt market scene to recognize arising patterns and troublesome powers that might reshape the business later on. This might include observing innovative headways, administrative changes, segment shifts, and other outer elements that could influence the market elements. By remaining sensitive to these patterns and expecting future turns of events, associations can situate themselves to benefit from arising amazing open doors and remain in front of the opposition.

In addition, associations can draw in with clients, accomplices, and different partners to accumulate criticism and experiences into their advancing requirements and inclinations. By encouraging open channels of correspondence and effectively requesting criticism from key partners, associations can acquire important bits of knowledge that illuminate their development endeavors and guarantee that their answers are lined up with market interest.

In synopsis, recognizing potential open doors for disturbance is a complex cycle that requires a profound comprehension of the market scene, compassion for the necessities of target clients, and premonition into future patterns and improvements. By utilizing methods, for example, market examination, plan thinking, and partner commitment, associations can reveal chances to enhance and make esteem in manners that rock the boat and drive significant change inside their ventures.

Planning a Problematic Plan of Action:

When open doors for disturbance have been recognized, the

subsequent stage is to plan a plan of action that gains from those potential open doors and empowers associations to make and catch esteem in imaginative ways. Planning a problematic plan of action includes reevaluating conventional ways to deal with esteem creation, income age, and client commitment, with an emphasis on conveying interesting and convincing arrangements that separate the association from contenders.

At the core of a troublesome plan of action lies a convincing offer that addresses neglected needs or problem areas in the market in a way that is essentially not the same as existing arrangements. This might include offering a fundamentally new item or administration, rethinking the client experience, or utilizing innovation to make new wellsprings of significant worth. By zeroing in on conveying esteem that is genuinely separated and convincing, associations can make serious areas of strength for disturbance and separation on the lookout.

As well as characterizing a convincing incentive, planning a problematic plan of action likewise includes deciding how worth will be caught and adapted. This might require reconsidering conventional income models and investigating elective methodologies, for example, membership-based evaluation, freemium models, or result-based estimation. By adjusting the income model to reflect the worth conveyed to clients, associations can make a maintainable and versatile plan of action that drives long-term achievement.

Besides, planning a troublesome plan of action includes distinguishing the best conveyance channels for arriving at target clients and conveying esteem. This might include utilizing computerized channels like internet business stages, virtual entertainment, and versatile applications to arrive at clients straightforwardly or cooperating with existing dissemination organizations to get to new business sectors and client fragments. By picking the right appropriation channels and improving the client venture, associations can boost their range and effect on the market.

Besides, planning a problematic course of action requires careful consideration of the hierarchical capacities and assets expected to really execute the technique. This might include putting resources into an innovation framework, ability securing and advancement, and associations or unions that supplement and improve the association's capacities. By adjusting the association's assets to its essential targets and plan of action, pioneers can guarantee that the association is strategically set up to execute its problematic technique and drive manageable development and achievement.

In outline, planning a problematic plan of action is a mind-boggling and iterative cycle that requires imagination, prescience, and key reasoning. By zeroing in on conveying a convincing offer, rethinking income age and circulation channels, and adjusting hierarchical capacities to key targets, associations can make a plan of action that rocks the boat, drives significant change, and gives them a manageable upper hand on the lookout.

Testing and repeating:

When a problematic plan of action has been planned, the next pivotal step is to test and emphasize the model to approve suppositions, assemble input, and refine techniques. This iterative way to deal with development is fundamental for guaranteeing that the plan of action is suitable, adaptable, and equipped for conveying worth to clients and partners over the long haul.

Testing a problematic plan of action includes directing trials and pilots to approve key presumptions and speculations based on the model. This might include sending off a base feasible item (MVP) or model to test market interest, leading A/B testing to assess different valuation or conveyance techniques, or running test case projects to evaluate client reaction and conduct. By efficiently testing various parts of the plan of action, associations can assemble experimental proof to illuminate independent directions and refine their procedures in light of certifiable criticism.

Besides, testing a problematic plan of action requires an eagerness to embrace vulnerability and gain from disappointment. Few out of every odd analysis will yield the ideal outcomes, and mishaps and difficulties are inescapable enroute. Notwithstanding, by embracing an outlook of trial and error and learning, associations can transform disappointment into important bits of knowledge that illuminate future emphases and at last lead to progress. This requires creating a culture that celebrates trial and error, supports risk-taking, and rewards gaining from mistakes.

Besides, emphasizing a problematic plan of action includes dissecting the consequences of tests and integrating input into the plan of the model. This might include refining the incentive in light of client criticism, changing valuing or circulation techniques in light of market elements, or turning to another methodology out and out in the event that underlying suppositions end up being imperfect. By consistently repeating the model in view of true criticism, associations can refine their methodologies and improve the probability of accomplishment after some time.

Besides, repeating a problematic plan of action includes examining the consequences of investigations and integrating criticism into the plan of the model. This might include refining the incentive in light of client criticism, changing evaluating or dissemination systems in view of market elements, or turning to another methodology through and through in the event that underlying suppositions end up being defective. By persistently repeating the model in light of certifiable criticism, associations can refine their systems and improve the probability of accomplishment over the long run.

In the rundown, testing and repeating a troublesome plan of action is fundamental to guaranteeing its reasonability and outcome. By methodically testing suppositions, embracing vulnerability and gaining from disappointment, and integrating criticism into the plan of the model, associations can refine their techniques, drive advancement, and make reasonable upper hand on the lookout.

Scaling and maintaining:

Scaling a problematic plan of action includes extending its range, effect, and benefit to catch a larger portion of the market and drive manageable development over the long haul. While starting achievements might be accomplished through limited-scope examinations and pilots, scaling requires an essential methodology that empowers associations to exploit early energy and open new doors for development.

One technique for scaling a troublesome plan of action is to use innovation and robotization to build proficiency and versatility. This might include putting resources into programming stages, information investigation devices, and different advancements that smooth out activities, further develop independent direction, and upgrade client encounters. By harnessing the force of innovation, associations can scale their tasks all the more quickly and cost-effectively, empowering them to enter new business sectors and serve a larger client base.

Besides, scaling a problematic plan of action requires an emphasis on building versatile foundations and capacities that can uphold development without forfeiting quality or client experience. This might include putting resources into versatile creation offices, extending appropriation organizations, and recruiting and preparing extra staff to fulfill developing needs. By proactively building limits and abilities in front of interest, associations can situate themselves for progress as they scale their activities.

Besides, scaling a troublesome plan of action requires a restrained way to deal with asset portions and prioritization. As associations develop, they might confront contending requests for assets and consideration, making it fundamental to center around drives that drive the best effect and convey the most worth to clients and partners. By focusing on ventures and drives in light of their essential arrangement and potential for development, associations can guarantee that they are actually dispensing assets and augmenting their profit from speculation.

Besides, supporting a problematic plan of action requires a guarantee of nonstop development and transformation to remain ahead of competitors and meet developing client needs. This might include routinely returning to and refining the plan of action in light of changing business sector elements, arising advancements, and moving client inclinations. By cultivating a culture of development and readiness, associations can stay responsive and versatile despite vulnerability and change, driving long-term achievement and intensity.

In synopsis, scaling and supporting a problematic plan of action is a multi-layered process that requires an essential methodology, restrained execution, and a guarantee of nonstop development. By utilizing innovation, building versatile foundations and capacities, focusing on asset distribution, and encouraging a culture of development and spryness, associations can scale their tasks effectively and drive reasonable development and seriousness on the lookout.

6

Chapter 6: Leveraging Technology for Innovation

Grasping the Job of Innovation in Advancement:

In the rapidly developing business scene, innovation fills in as an impetus for development, driving extraordinary change and reshaping ventures in significant ways. Understanding the job of innovation in development is fundamental for associations trying to remain serious and flourish in a computerized world. By investigating the convergence of innovation and development, associations can open new doors for development, separation, and value creation.

At its center, innovation empowers advancement by giving associations the instruments, assets, and abilities they need to foster new items, administrations, and plans of action that meet developing client needs and inclinations. From headways in man-made brainpower and AI to forward leaps in blockchain and the Web of Things, innovation has the ability to open new wellsprings of significant worth and drive disruption across basically every industry.

Besides, innovation has democratized access to development, evening the odds and engaging associations, all things considered, to contend on a worldwide scale. With the multiplication of distributed computing, open-source programming, and low-code improvement stages, associations can use state-of-the art advancements without the requirement for huge forthright speculation or particular aptitude. This democratization of development has democratized access to advancement, making everything fair and engaging associations, all things considered, to contend on a worldwide scale. With the multiplication of distributed computing, open-source programming, and low-code improvement stages, associations can use state-of-the art advancements without the requirement for huge forthright ventures or concentrated abilities. This democratization of development has democratized access to development, evening the odds and engaging associations, everything being equal, to contend on a worldwide scale. With the multiplication of distributed computing, open-source programming, and low-code advancement stages, associations can use state-of-the art innovations without the requirement for critical forthright speculation or particular ability. This democratization of advancement has opened up additional opportunities for joint effort and co-creation, empowering associations to team up with accomplices, clients, and different partners to drive development and make esteem in new and unforeseen ways.

Besides, innovation empowers associations to tackle the force of information and investigation to acquire bits of knowledge into client conduct, market patterns, and serious elements, illuminating more educated direction and driving more designated development endeavors. By utilizing information-driven experiences, associations can recognize arising open doors, expect market moves, and foster creative arrangements that meet the developing requirements of their clients.

In summary, understanding the role of innovation in advancement is fundamental for associations looking to drive significant change and remain serious in the present computerized world. By embracing innovation as an impetus for development, associations can open new doors for development, separation, and worth creation, engaging them to flourish in a time characterized by quick change and disturbance.

Outfitting Information and Examination:

In the period of computerized change, information has arisen as a strong driver of development, furnishing associations with uncommon bits of knowledge into client conduct, market patterns, and business execution. Tackling the force of information and investigation is fundamental for associations looking to remain on the ball and drive development that conveys unmistakable worth to clients and partners.

Information and examination assume a critical role in driving development by giving associations the data they need to settle on informed choices and recognize open doors for development and separation. By gathering, examining, and deciphering information from different sources, associations can acquire insights into client inclinations, market patterns, and serious elements, empowering them to foster imaginative arrangements that address neglected needs and gain by opening doors.

One of the critical advantages of outfitting information and examination for development is the capacity to reveal stowed-away examples and patterns that may not be evident through customary strategies for investigation. By utilizing advanced examination strategies, for example, AI and prescient demonstrating, associations can recognize relationships, exceptions, and irregularities in their information that might pave the way to opening new wellsprings of significant worth and driving advancement.

In addition, information and examination empower associations to gauge the effect of development drives all the more and arrive at information-driven conclusions about where to distribute assets and focus on endeavors. By following key execution pointers (KPIs) and measurements connected with advancement, associations can survey the outcome of their drives, distinguish regions for development, and emphasize their systems in view of continuous criticism.

Moreover, information and examination can play a pivotal role in encouraging a culture of trial and error and consistent improvement within associations. By furnishing workers with access to information and examination devices, associations can engage them to investigate groundbreaking thoughts, test theories, and repeat their development endeavors in an information-driven way. This iterative way to deal with development empowers associations to gain from disappointment, adjust their methodologies in light of experimental proof, and drive constant improvement and advancement after some time.

In summary, tackling information and examination is fundamental for associations trying to drive development and remain cutthroat in the present information-driven world. By utilizing the force of information to acquire bits of knowledge, go with informed choices, and cultivate a culture of trial and error, associations can open new doors for development, separation, and worth creation, situating themselves for long-term progress in an undeniably computerized and information-driven business scene.

Embracing Arising Advancements:

Advancement frequently blossoms with the reception and combination of emerging innovations that can possibly alter enterprises and change the manner in which associations work. Embracing these arising advances is fundamental for associations looking to remain on the ball and drive development that conveys genuine worth to clients and partners.

One class of arising advancements that holds critical commitment for development is vivid innovations, like increased reality (AR) and augmented reality (VR). These advancements have the ability to make vivid and intelligent encounters that obscure the lines between the physical and computerized universes, opening up additional opportunities for correspondence, coordinated effort, and commitment. Associations can use AR and VR to improve client encounters, smooth out business tasks, and drive advancement in regions like preparation, showcasing, and item improvement.

One more arising innovation with the possibility to drive development is 3D printing, otherwise called added substance fabricating. 3D printing empowers associations to make actual articles layer by layer from computerized plans, considering more prominent customization, adaptability, and effectiveness in the assembling system. By utilizing 3D printing innovation, associations can model new items all the more rapidly, produce uniquely designed products on request, and lessen waste and expenses related to customary assembly strategies.

Moreover, advancements like man-made brainpower (artificial intelligence) and AI can possibly change enterprises by empowering associations to computerize processes, break down information at scale, and determine bits of knowledge that drive development. Simulated intelligence-fueled calculations can reveal stowed-away examples and patterns in information, distinguish potential open doors for enhancement and improvement, and even produce clever fixes to complex issues. By embracing artificial intelligence and AI, associations can open new doors for advancement in regions, for example, through prescient examination, customized proposals, and savvy mechanization.

Besides, blockchain innovation has arisen as a problematic power in businesses, for example, in finance, production networks, and medical care, offering additional opportunities for straightforwardness, security, and productivity. Blockchain empowers associations to make carefully designed, decentralized records of exchanges, killing the need for middlemen and empowering new models of trust and cooperation. By utilizing blockchain innovation, associations can smooth out processes, lessen expenses, and drive development in regions, for example, production network discernibility, computerized personality among executives, and secure exchanges.

In outline, embracing arising advances is fundamental for associations looking to drive development and remain cutthroat in the rapidly advancing business scene. By utilizing advancements, for example, AR and VR, 3D printing, artificial intelligence and AI, and blockchain, associations can open new doors for development, separation, and worth creation, situating themselves for outcome in an undeniably computerized and interconnected world.

Encouraging a Culture of Trial and Error:

Key to driving development through innovation is cultivating a culture inside associations that energizes trial and error, risk-taking, and gaining from disappointment. This culture of trial and error is fundamental for empowering representatives to investigate novel thoughts, test speculations, and push the limits of what's conceivable with arising advancements.

One of the critical parts of cultivating a culture of trial and error is establishing a climate where workers feel empowered to face challenges and seek out inventive thoughts unafraid of disappointment. This expects initiative to convey a reasonable message that trial and error isn't just supported, but in addition celebrated for driving advancement and development. By creating mental security and eliminating obstructions to trial and error, associations can create a culture where representatives feel happy venturing outside their usual ranges of familiarity and investigating additional opportunities.

Besides, encouraging a culture of trial and error requires giving representatives the important assets, devices, and backing to transform their thoughts into the real world. This might include putting resources into an innovation framework, giving access to information and investigation instruments, and offering preparation and advancement valuable chances to fabricate abilities and capacities connected with arising innovations. By furnishing representatives with the assets they need to analyze and develop, associations can engage them to drive significant change and create an incentive for the association.

Besides, cultivating a culture of trial and error includes laying out cycles and structures for overseeing development drives and gaining from trial and error. This might include embracing certain procedures, plan-thinking approaches, or lean startup standards to direct advancement endeavors and emphasize thinking rapidly and productively. By embracing iterative, information-driven ways to deal with development, associations can limit risk and boost the probability of achievement, even despite vulnerability and equivocalness.

Moreover, encouraging a culture of trial and error expects pioneers to show others how it was done and exhibit their obligation to development and learning. This might include effectively taking part in development drives, empowering workers to share their thoughts and bits of knowledge, commending victories, and learning potential open doors enroute. By demonstrating the ways of behaving and mentalities related to trial and error and learning, pioneers can create a culture that values development and drives ceaseless improvement and development.

In summary, encouraging a culture of trial and error is fundamental for associations trying to drive development through innovation. By establishing a climate where workers feel engaged to face challenges, furnishing them with the assets and backing they need to explore and master, laying out cycles and systems for overseeing development, and showing others how it is done, associations can create a culture that cultivates imagination, development, and constant improvement, driving long-term achievement and seriousness in the computerized age.

Conquering Difficulties and Dangers

While utilizing innovation for development offers gigantic open doors, it likewise gives associations a remarkable arrangement of difficulties and dangers that should be explored successfully to understand the maximum capacity of advancement drives. Understanding and addressing these difficulties is fundamental for associations looking to drive development through innovation in a reasonable and mindful way.

One of the essential difficulties related to utilizing innovation for advancement is network protection dangers and information security concerns. As associations progressively depend on innovation to gather, store, and dissect information, they become more helpless against cyberattacks, information breaks, and other security dangers. Also, guidelines like the Overall Information Assurance Guideline (GDPR) and the California Shopper Security Act (CCPA) force severe necessities on associations in regards to the assortment, use, and insurance of individual information. By putting resources into strong network safety measures, carrying out information security best practices, and remaining consistent with pertinent guidelines, associations can relieve these dangers and shield themselves and their clients from likely damage.

Besides, moral contemplations pose a potential threat to the reception and organization of arising innovations, especially those with the potential for critical cultural effect, like man-made reasoning and biotechnology. Concerns connected with predisposition, decency, responsibility, and straightforwardness should be painstakingly thought of and addressed to guarantee that innovation is utilized mindfully and morally. By laying out moral rules, leading exhaustive gamble appraisals, and drawing in with partners to comprehend their interests and points of view, associations can alleviate moral dangers and construct entrust with clients, representatives, and the more extensive local area.

Besides, innovation reception boundaries, for example, protection from change, absence of specialized mastery, and social latency, can obstruct advancement endeavors and ruin associations' capacity to understand the advantages of innovation completely. By putting resources into change the board drives, giving preparation and backing to representatives, and encouraging a culture of receptiveness and versatility, associations can defeat these boundaries and establish a climate that embraces development and innovation-enabled change.

Also, the fast speed of mechanical change and the vulnerability inborn in arising advances can present difficulties for associations trying to settle on informed speculation choices and focus on development drives successfully. By remaining informed about mechanical turns of events, leading exhaustive statistical surveying, and drawing in with outer accomplices and specialists, associations can arrive at additional educated conclusions about where to contribute their assets and center their advancement endeavors.

In synopsis, beating difficulties and dangers related to utilizing innovation for advancement is fundamental for associations trying to drive supportable development and seriousness in the computerized age. By tending to online protection dangers and information security concerns, exploring moral contemplations, defeating innovation reception boundaries, and remaining informed about the mechanical turns of events, associations can moderate dangers and open the maximum capacity of innovation-enabled development, driving long-haul achievement and worth creation.

7

Chapter 7: Overcoming Challenges in the Innovation Journey

Distinguishing Normal Difficulties:

Leaving on the development venture is a thrilling undertaking, yet it's not without its share of obstacles and deterrents. To explore this way effectively, it's pivotal to initially distinguish and comprehend the normal difficulties that associations experience enroute. These difficulties can appear in different structures, from interior protection from outer market influences to tending to them head-on, which is fundamental for supporting energy and driving significant change.

One pervasive test that associations face is the inclination to focus on momentary increases over long-haul advancement. In a world driven by quarterly outcomes and prompt returns, it's not difficult to become consumed by the tensions of the present and neglect to focus on the need to put resources into future development and maintainability. Beating this challenge requires a change in outlook, with pioneers and leaders perceiving the worth of long-haul development and focusing on dispensing assets and consideration as needed.

Also, hierarchical storehouses and obstructions to cooperation can block advancement endeavors by smothering inventiveness and restraining the free progression of thoughts. At the point when various divisions and groups work in segregation, open doors for cross-fertilization and synergistic development are lost, prompting repetitive endeavors and botched open doors. Separating these storehouses and encouraging a culture of cooperation and information sharing is fundamental for opening the maximum capacity for development inside associations.

Besides, an absence of clear bearing and arrangement with key targets can hamper development endeavors by creating equivocalness and vulnerability about needs and objectives. Without a mutual perspective of where the association is going and the way that development squeezes into the more extensive key system, groups might battle to focus on drives and designate assets. Adjusting advancement endeavors to key goals requires clear correspondence, the arrangement of motivating forces, and a standard reassessment of needs to guarantee that development drives are driving worth and propelling the association's main goal.

Furthermore, hazard avoidance and a feeling of dread toward disappointment can smother development by putting trial and error and inventive reasoning down. In a culture that punishes missteps and prizes congruity, workers might wonder whether or not to face challenges and seek after striking thoughts, selecting rather for the security of the state of affairs. Conquering this challenge expects pioneers to establish a climate that celebrates trial and error, embraces disappointment as a learning opportunity, and prizes drive and development.

In synopsis, distinguishing and understanding the normal difficulties that associations face in the development venture is fundamental to conquering them and driving significant change. By perceiving the propensity to focus on momentary increases, separating hierarchical storehouses, adjusting development endeavors to vital goals, and cultivating a culture of trial and error and hazard-taking, associations can conquer these difficulties and open the maximum capacity of advancement to drive long-haul development and seriousness.

Building a Culture of Development:
Fundamental to defeating difficulties in the development venture is the development of a culture that values and supports development at each level of the association. A culture of development cultivates a climate where inventiveness, trial and error, and cooperation are empowered, empowering people and groups to investigate groundbreaking thoughts, proceed with well-balanced plans of action, and push the limits of what's conceivable. Building such a culture requires purposeful exertion and responsibility from initiative to create the circumstances that support development.

One critical part of building a culture of development is encouraging mental wellbeing, where people feel open to facing challenges, offering disagreeing viewpoints, and stirring things up unafraid of revenge or judgment. At the point when representatives have a solid sense of security to voice their thoughts and examination with new methodologies, development twists and forward leaps are bound to happen. Pioneers assume a critical role in promoting mental wellbeing by displaying receptiveness, weakness, and modesty and by effectively reassuring different viewpoints and useful criticism.

Besides, building a culture of development requires furnishing representatives with the independence, assets, and backing they need to enhance and investigate. This might include apportioning devoted time and assets for advancement projects, giving admittance to preparing and improving valuable open doors, and perceiving and remunerating creative ways of behaving and commitments. By enabling representatives to take responsibility for thoughts and seek after them with enthusiasm and conviction, associations can release the full inventive capability of their labor force and drive significant change.

Moreover, building a culture of development includes making designs and cycles that work with age, assessing, and executing groundbreaking thoughts. This might incorporate laying out cross-useful groups, advancement labs, or hatcheries committed to investigating and creating inventive answers for key difficulties. By giving an organized system to development, associations can channel inventiveness and joint effort toward taking care of genuine issues and driving incentives for clients and partners.

Moreover, incorporating a culture of development requires inserting development into the association's DNA, making it a central piece of its personality and values. This might include integrating advancement into execution measurements and objectives, incorporating development into worker onboarding and preparing programs, and commending triumphs and learning open doors connected with development. By regulating development as a central part of the association's way of life, pioneers can guarantee that it stays a need and concentrates even despite contending requests and tensions.

In summary, fabricating a culture of development is fundamental for defeating difficulties in the development process and driving significant change inside associations. By cultivating mental wellbeing, engaging representatives, making designs and cycles that help development, and implanting advancement into the association's DNA, chiefs can establish a climate where imagination flourishes and advancement prospers, empowering the association to adjust, develop, and flourish in an undeniably mind-boggling and dynamic business scene.

Adjusting Advancement to Vital Goals:

One of the principal challenges associations face in their advancement process is guaranteeing an arrangement between development endeavors and the overall key targets of the association. Without this arrangement, development drives might need heading, neglect to address basic business needs, and, at last, battle to convey significant effect. Consequently, associations must lay out a clear arrangement among advancement and key targets to expand the value produced from development ventures.

To accomplish arrangements, associations should initially express their essential goals and recognize the key regions where development can drive esteem and contribute to accomplishing those targets. This requires a profound comprehension of the association's central goal, vision, and values, as well as its cutthroat scene, market elements, and client needs. By plainly characterizing vital targets and needs, associations can give a reasonable guide to development endeavors and guarantee that they are centered around tending to the most squeezing difficulties and potential open doors confronting the association.

Also, associations should lay out systems for continuous correspondence and coordinated effort between advancement groups and key partners across the association. This might include normal gatherings, studios, or cross-useful teams devoted to adjusting development endeavors to vital goals and guaranteeing that advancement drives are firmly incorporated with more extensive business needs. By cultivating a culture of cooperation and mutual perspective, associations can guarantee that development endeavors are lined up with key targets and have the help and purchase of key partners.

Besides, associations should lay out measurements and KPIs to gauge the progress of advancement drives and track progress toward key targets. These measurements ought to be lined up with the association's essential needs and mirror the ideal results of development endeavors, like income development, cost investment funds, consumer loyalty, or a portion of the overall industry. By laying out clear measurements for progress, associations can screen the effect of advancement drives, distinguish regions for development, and come to information-driven conclusions about where to distribute assets and focus on endeavors.

Moreover, associations should make an administration plan to supervise development endeavors and guarantee that they stay aligned with vital goals. This might include laying out an advancement board or directing a council that involves senior pioneers from across the association liable for defining boundaries, distributing assets, and giving oversight and direction to development groups. By laying out clear responsibility and administration systems, associations can guarantee that advancement endeavors are lined up with key goals and have really figured out how to convey their greatest worth.

In synopsis, adjusting advancement to key goals is fundamental for associations trying to drive significant change and gain a manageable upper hand. By articulating clear essential targets, cultivating cooperation and correspondence, laying out measurements for progress, and making an administration design to supervise development endeavors, associations can guarantee that development drives are lined up with more extensive business needs and situated for outcome in accomplishing vital goals.

Beating Protection from Change:

Protection from change is an unavoidable test that associations experience in their development process. People are normally disposed to oppose change because of dread of the obscure, loss of control, and gambles related to leaving recognizable schedules and practices. In any case, defeating protection from change is fundamental for driving development and cultivating a culture of ceaseless improvement inside associations.

One of the vital procedures for beating protection from change is to convey a convincing vision for the future and the reasoning behind the proposed changes. By articulating an unmistakable and convincing vision that features the advantages of development and the open doors it presents for the association and its partners, chiefs can rouse certainty and construct support for change. Besides, by making sense of the explanations for the requirement for change and tending to worries and protests proactively, pioneers can assist with reducing fears and vulnerabilities and creating a need to get moving and reason around development drives.

Moreover, including workers in the change cycle and requesting their feedback and criticism can assist with expanding purchase-in and responsibility for proposed changes. At the point when representatives feel that their voices are heard and that they have a stake in forming the fate of the association, they are bound to embrace change and effectively add to its prosperity. This might include drawing in workers in meetings to generate new ideas, center gatherings, or municipal events to accumulate thoughts, address concerns, and co-make arrangements cooperatively.

Moreover, offering help and assets for workers to explore the change interaction can assist with diminishing obstruction and achieving smoother progress. This might incorporate contribution preparation and improvement chances to construct abilities and capacities connected with advancement, giving instruction and tutoring to assist representatives with adjusting to better approaches for working, and making discussions for sharing prescribed procedures and examples gained from effective development drives. By furnishing workers with the devices, assets, and backing they need to prevail despite change, associations can relieve obstruction and speed up the speed of advancement.

Besides, commending victories and perceiving the commitments of workers who embrace change can assist with building up certain ways of behaving and encourage a culture that values development and variation. By freely recognizing and remunerating people and groups who show receptiveness, nimbleness, and strength notwithstanding change, pioneers can create a feeling of force and fervor around development drives, spurring others to stick to this same pattern.

In synopsis, defeating protection from change is fundamental for driving development and encouraging a culture of persistent improvement inside associations. By imparting a convincing vision for the future, including representatives in the change cycle, offering help and assets, and praising triumphs, pioneers can establish a climate where change is embraced as a chance for development as opposed to dreaded as a danger to business as usual.

Exploring Asset Requirements:

Asset requirements represent a huge test for associations looking to drive development, as restricted spending plans, ability deficiencies, and contending needs can obstruct the capacity to put resources into development drives and carry groundbreaking plans to completion. Be that as it may, exploring these imperatives requires innovativeness, vital reasoning, and an eagerness to investigate elective ways to deal with development.

One technique for exploring asset requirements is to focus on development drives that offer the best potential for effect and profit from ventures. By zeroing in on drives that adjust intimately with vital goals and can possibly convey unmistakable advantages concerning income development, cost reserve funds, or consumer loyalty, associations can boost the worth produced from restricted assets and guarantee that advancement endeavors are coordinated toward the most encouraging open doors.

Also, associations can use outside organizations and coordinated efforts to increase their inside abilities and access extra assets and mastery. By cooperating with new businesses, scholastic foundations, research associations, or different organizations in correlative enterprises, associations can take advantage of novel thoughts, advancements, and ability pools that they might not approach inside. These associations can assist associations with conquering asset imperatives by sharing expenses, dangers, and rewards and speeding up the speed of advancement through cooperation.

Moreover, associations can embrace lean and nimble techniques to smooth out advancement processes and decrease waste and failure. By embracing an outlook of trial and error and cycle, associations can test thoughts rapidly and cost-effectively, gain from disappointment, and emphasize their methodologies in light of criticism and information. This iterative way to deal with advancement empowers associations to preserve assets and limit risk while boosting the probability of progress.

Also, associations can use innovation to democratize access to advancement and lower the barriers to cooperation. Distributed computing, open-source programming, and low-code improvement stages empower associations to create and convey imaginative arrangements more rapidly and cost-really than any time in recent memory, diminishing the requirement for enormous forthright interests in foundation and innovation. By embracing innovation as an empowering agent of development, associations can defeat asset limitations and open new doors for development and separation.

In synopsis, exploring asset imperatives is a test that associations should address proactively to drive development and stay serious in the present speedy business climate. By focusing on drives, utilizing outer associations, taking on lean and light approaches, and embracing innovation, associations can conquer asset requirements and open the maximum capacity of development to drive long-haul achievement and worth creation.

8

Chapter 8: The Future of Innovation

Arising Patterns in Development:

As we look into the distance of development, it's obvious that the scene is ceaselessly advancing, molded by a heap of arising patterns that hold the commitment of changing enterprises and reshaping the manner in which associations work. Investigating these patterns offers important bits of knowledge for the future course of development, furnishing associations with the foreknowledge they need to adjust and flourish in an always evolving climate.

Among the most eminent patterns driving development is the quick headway of innovation, which keeps on advancing at a remarkable speed. From man-made brainpower and AI to blockchain and quantum figuring, these state-of-the art advances are opening new outskirts of plausibility, empowering associations to mechanize processes, break down information at scale, and foster imaginative answers for complex difficulties. Understanding the capability of these advancements and how they can be applied to address business needs is fundamental for associations looking to remain on the ball and tackle the force of development to drive development and intensity.

Moreover, changing shopper ways of behaving and market elements are reshaping the development scene, setting out new open doors and difficulties for associations across ventures. The ascent of the computerized economy, the shift towards remote work and internet business, and the developing interest in customized encounters are only a couple of instances of patterns that are impacting the way in which associations improve and draw in with clients. By remaining sensitive to these moving patterns and adjusting development endeavors to advance client needs and inclinations, associations can situate themselves for outcome later on and keep up with significance in a quickly evolving commercial center.

Besides, the ascent of interconnectedness and globalization is encouraging more prominent cooperation and information sharing across borders, empowering associations to take advantage of an abundance of different points of view, thoughts, and mastery. From open development drives and publicly supporting stages to cross-line organizations and biological systems, associations are embracing cooperation as an essential basic for driving development and remaining cutthroat in an interconnected world. By cultivating a culture of transparency, joint effort, and co-creation, associations can use the aggregate insight of their organizations to produce novel thoughts, tackle complex issues, and drive significant change.

In outline, understanding arising patterns in development is fundamental for associations looking to explore the future scene and drive significant change. By remaining informed about mechanical headways, changing buyer ways of behaving, and worldwide patterns, associations can expect open doors and difficulties, adjust their procedures likewise, and position themselves as pioneers in the steadily advancing universe of advancement.

The Job of Troublesome Advancements:

At the core of things to come in development lies the extraordinary force of troublesome advances. These momentous headways, going from man-made consciousness and blockchain to biotechnology and quantum processing, are reshaping enterprises, reclassifying plans of action, and changing the manner in which associations work.

Understanding the crucial role that problematic advancements play in driving development is fundamental for associations trying to outfit their true capacity and gain an upper hand in the quick-moving computerized scene of tomorrow.

Man-made brainpower (simulated intelligence) and AI, for example, have arisen as incredible assets for computerizing processes, examining tremendous measures of information, and uncovering experiences that were already distant. From prescient examination and customized suggestions to independent vehicles and remote helpers, man-made intelligence-driven advancements are changing ventures and opening new doors for development and proficiency. Associations that influence man-made intelligence really can acquire a critical benefit as far as dynamic speed, functional greatness, and client experience, situating themselves as pioneers in their separate fields.

Also, blockchain innovation has caught the creative minds of businesses, going from money and inventory networks across the board to medical care and then some, offering the commitment of more prominent straightforwardness, security, and effectiveness. By giving carefully designed, decentralized records of exchanges, blockchain empowers associations to smooth out processes, lessen expenses, and upgrade trust and straightforwardness across their environments. Whether it's following the provenance of merchandise, getting advanced personalities, or working with distributed exchanges, blockchain-controlled developments are reshaping the manner in which associations direct business and collaborate with partners.

In addition, biotechnology is driving forward leaps in medical services, horticulture, and natural supportability, offering creative answers for a portion of mankind's most squeezing difficulties. From quality-altering and customized medication to biofuels and economical horticulture rehearsals, biotechnology is opening additional opportunities for working on human wellbeing, improving food security, and safeguarding the planet. Associations that put resources into biotechnology advancement can situate themselves as pioneers in their businesses and make significant commitments to society and the climate.

In summary, the job of troublesome advances in driving development couldn't possibly be more significant. From man-made brainpower and blockchain to biotechnology and then some, these extraordinary headways are reshaping enterprises, empowering associations to open new doors, and creating an incentive for clients and partners. By embracing problematic advances and utilizing their true capacity, associations can remain on the ball, drive significant change, and flourish in the dynamic and questionable scene representing things to come.

Developing for supportability:

As we peer into the eventual fate of development, one topic arises as both an ethical goal and an essential need: supportability. The squeezing ecological, social, and financial difficulties confronting our planet request creative arrangements that offset success with planetary well-being, guaranteeing that people in the future can flourish in a world that is impartial, strong, and feasible. Enhancing maintainability expects associations to reconsider their ways to deal with item advancement, store network executives, and partner commitment, putting natural and social contemplations at the forefront of their dynamic cycles.

One region where development holds massive commitments for manageability is sustainable power. From sun-oriented and wind-oriented capacity to hydroelectric and geothermal energy, environmentally friendly power sources offer perfect, plentiful options in contrast to petroleum products that can assist with lessening ozone-depleting substance discharges, alleviating environmental change, and advancing energy freedom. By putting resources into sustainable power advances and frameworks, associations might not just diminish their ecological impression at any point yet additionally set out new open doors for financial development and occupation creation in networks all over the planet.

Moreover, the progress toward a roundabout economy addresses a change in perspective in the way we configure, produce, and consume labor and products. As opposed to following a direct "take-make-arrange" model, a round economy means to save assets being used to the extent that this would be possible, separating the most extreme worth from them while limiting waste and contamination. Developments, for example, item as-a-service models, reusing and remanufacturing innovations, and supportable materials are driving the progress toward a roundabout economy, empowering associations to lessen costs, improve asset effectiveness, and create an incentive for clients and society.

Also, social-effect financial planning and capable money are emerging as useful assets for driving positive change and propelling maintainability objectives. By coordinating natural, social, and administrative (ESG) models into venture choices, associations can adjust their monetary advantages to their qualities, supporting drives that convey both monetary returns and social or ecological advantages. From green securities and effect assets to reasonable money management procedures, there is a developing cluster of monetary instruments and vehicles accessible to associations trying to prepare capital for economic turn of events.

Also, a dependable store network on the board is fundamental for associations looking to improve supportability all through their value chains. By working intimately with providers to further develop work rehearsals, diminish natural effects, and advance moral obtaining, associations can relieve gambles, fabricate trust with clients and partners, and make a more feasible and strong inventory network. For example, blockchain innovation is additionally empowering more noteworthy straightforwardness and discernibility in supply chains, permitting associations to follow the excursion of items from source to destination and guaranteeing that they satisfy thorough manageability guidelines.

In outline, improving maintainability is fundamental for associations trying to flourish from here on out and make a world that is prosperous, impartial, and economical for all. By putting resources into sustainable power, progressing to a round economy, embracing social effect, effective money management, and advancing dependable store networks, executives and associations can drive significant change and have a beneficial outcome on society and the planet. Through development, we have the ability to construct a superior future for a long time into the future.

The Ascent of Open Development:

In the developing stage of development, the idea of open advancement has arisen as a strong change in outlook, testing customary thoughts of advancement as an inside, shut entryway process. Open development perceives that important thoughts, information, and skills exist both inside and beyond associations and that by taking advantage of outside wellsprings of development, associations can speed up the speed of advancement, diminish expenses, and access a more extensive pool of abilities and assets.

At its center, open development is about joint effort, sharing, and co-creation. As opposed to depending entirely on interior research and development divisions to create thoughts and foster arrangements, associations are making their way for outside accomplices, including clients, providers, research organizations, new companies, and even contenders, to partake in the advancement cycle. By utilizing the aggregate insight and capacities of a different environment of partners, associations can get to an abundance of thoughts, bits of knowledge, and mastery that would be troublesome, in the event that certainly feasible, to inside repeat.

One of the vital advantages of open development is its capacity to speed up the speed of advancement by utilizing outer wellsprings of information and skill. By taking advantage of the aggregate knowledge of a worldwide organization of partners, associations can get to groundbreaking thoughts and points of view, distinguish arising patterns and valuable open doors, and remain on the ball in quickly developing business sectors. In addition, open advancement empowers associations to diminish the time and cost of development by sharing dangers, assets, and compensations with outer accomplices, permitting them to put up creative answers for sale to the public more rapidly and effectively than through customary research and development.

Besides, open development cultivates a culture of receptiveness, coordinated effort, and information sharing inside associations, separating storehouses and boundaries to correspondence and creating a more unique and spry development environment. By empowering workers to team up with outer accomplices, share thoughts and bits of knowledge, and gain from others, associations can cultivate a culture that values trial and error, innovativeness, and consistent improvement, driving development at each level of the association.

Additionally, open development empowers associations to access specific abilities and assets that may not be accessible inside. By joining forces with new companies, scholarly foundations, research associations, and other outside partners, associations can take advantage of state-of-the art innovations, research abilities, and industry mastery that supplement their own assets and capacities. These associations can empower associations to foster imaginative arrangements more rapidly and successfully than they could all alone, giving them an upper hand in the commercial center.

In summary, the ascent of open advancement is changing the manner in which associations approach development, testing customary models, and opening new doors for coordinated effort, imagination, and worth creation. By embracing open development standards and practices, associations can access a more extensive pool of abilities and assets, speed up the speed of advancement, cultivate a culture of joint effort and learning, and gain a strategic advantage in an undeniably interconnected and dynamic business scene. Through open development, associations can possibly drive significant change and provide an incentive for clients, partners, and society in general.

Developing a Culture of Consistent Development

As we ponder the eventual fate of development, one thing turns out to be crystal clear: advancement isn't an objective but rather an excursion—aa progressing, iterative course of investigation, trial and error, and transformation. Developing a culture of consistent advancement is fundamental for associations trying to flourish in an undeniably unique and unsure business climate, where the capacity to adjust, advance, and enhance quickly is the way to long-term achievement.

At the core of a culture of consistent development lies an outlook of interest, transparency, and versatility—an eagerness to scrutinize the state of affairs, investigate groundbreaking thoughts, and embrace change as a chance for development and learning. Associations that encourage this attitude engage their representatives to challenge regular reasoning, explore different avenues regarding new methodologies, and go ahead with potentially dangerous courses of action in quest for imaginative answers to complex issues.

Besides, a culture of consistent development is portrayed by a persevering spotlight on client necessities and inclinations, driving associations to remain sensitive to developing business sector patterns, expect future requests, and proactively search out chances to make an incentive for clients. By putting the client at the focal point of the development cycle, associations can guarantee that their endeavors are lined up with market necessities and that their developments genuinely affect the existence of their clients.

Moreover, a culture of persistent development flourishes with co-operation, collaboration, and variety of thought, perceiving that the most weighty thoughts frequently arise out of the convergence of alternate points of view and teaching. By encouraging a climate where representatives from assorted foundations and encounters meet up to share thoughts, challenge presumptions, and co-make arrangements, associations can release the full inventive capability of their groups and drive advancement at each level of the association.

Moreover, a culture of consistent development embraces trial and error and cycles as fundamental parts of the development interaction, perceiving that disappointment isn't just unavoidable but in addition vital for learning and development. Associations that support trial and error engage their workers to face challenges, test speculations, and gain from the two triumphs and disappointments, empowering them to emphasize their thoughts, refine their methodologies, and, at last, convey more inventive answers for the market.

In the rundown, developing a culture of constant advancement is fundamental for associations looking to flourish in store for advance-ment. By cultivating a mentality of interest, transparency, and strength, putting the client at the focal point of the development cycle, encouraging cooperation and variety of thought, and embracing trial and error and emphasis, associations can establish a climate where development twists, and they can adjust, advance, and prevail in a consistently impacting world. Through a culture of constant development, associations have the ability to drive significant change, open new doors, and make a superior future for themselves and society as a whole.

Conclusion:

Recap of Key Experiences:

As we get closer to our investigation of the development of the computerized age, it's fundamental to ponder the critical bits of knowledge and illustrations advanced all through this excursion. From digging into the problematic powers molding enterprises to revealing procedures for exploring the intricacies of the advancement scene, every section has offered significant points of view and noteworthy experiences for associations trying to flourish in a time characterized by fast change and vulnerability.

At the core of our investigation lies the acknowledgement that disturbance isn't only a danger to be dreaded but additionally a potential chance to be seized. By grasping the drivers of disturbance and embracing a mentality of readiness, versatility, and flexibility, associations can situate themselves to make due as well as flourish despite vulnerability. Besides, by utilizing arising innovations, embracing open development, and cultivating a culture of constant learning and trial and error, associations can open additional opportunities, drive significant change, and create an incentive for clients and partners.

All through our excursion, we've likewise investigated the significance of adjusting development endeavors to vital targets, cultivating a culture of cooperation and inventiveness, and conquering protection from change. These experiences highlight the significance of authority support, hierarchical arrangement, and a promise to development as basic achievement factors for associations trying to drive significant change and make economical upper hand in the present speedy computerized scene.

As we finish up our investigation, let us not fail to remember that development isn't an objective but rather an excursion—an excursion set apart by vulnerability, intricacy, and an unfathomable open door. By embracing the test of development, staying inquisitive, receptive, and proactive in searching out novel thoughts and potential open doors, and focusing on encouraging a culture that values trial and error, imagination, and cooperation, we can chart a course towards a future characterized by development, strength, and flourishing.

Source of inspiration:

As we close our excursion through the domains of development in the advanced age, making an interpretation of our freshly discovered bits of knowledge right into it is basic. The information and viewpoints acquired from this investigation act as a compass, directing us towards the following stages of our development process. Subsequently, I welcome you, dear peruser, to set out on an excursion of change and development regarding the source of inspiration introduced here.

Let us, most importantly, perceive that the computerized age requests dexterity, versatility, and a readiness to embrace change. It isn't sufficient to just recognize the significance of development; we should effectively focus on cultivating a culture that values and focuses on it. As pioneers, chiefs, and change specialists inside our associations, we have an obligation to support development as an essential objective, driving drives that rock the boat and impel our associations forward.

Besides, let us not underestimate the force of joint effort and aggregate knowledge in driving advancement. By separating storehouses, cultivating cross-practical cooperation, and drawing in with outer accomplices and partners, we can get to an abundance of different viewpoints, thoughts, and mastery that can fuel our development endeavors and speed up our advancement towards our objectives. Allow us to use the force of open development to take advantage of the aggregate insight of the group and co-make arrangements that address the most squeezing difficulties confronting our associations and society as a whole.

Moreover, let us focus on constant learning and improvement as people and associations. The speed of progress in advanced age is perseverance, and the best way to remain on the ball is to stay inquisitive, receptive, and proactive in searching out novel thoughts, bits of knowledge, and potential open doors. Allow us to embrace an outlook of long-lasting learning, continually provoking ourselves to develop, adjust, and advance in light of changing conditions and arising patterns.

All in all, let us notice the source of inspiration introduced here and find proactive ways to drive advancement in our associations and networks. By embracing change, encouraging joint effort, and focusing on constant learning and improvement, we can chart a course towards a future characterized by development, versatility, and success. Together, let us jump all over the chances that lie ahead and release the maximum capacity of development to make a superior world for a long time into the future.

Significance of Persistent Learning:

In the consistently developing scene of advancement, one thing stays steady: the significance of persistent learning. As we explore the intricacies of the computerized age, the speed of progress is speeding up, and the best way to remain on the ball is to embrace a mentality of deep-rooted learning and variation. This excursion of consistent learning isn't just fundamental for individual and expert development; it is additionally basic for driving advancement and remaining cutthroat in the present speedy world.

By focusing on persistent learning, we can stay up-to-date with the most recent patterns, advancements, and best practices for forming our ventures and callings. Whether it's dominating new abilities, keeping up to date with arising patterns, or investigating creative thoughts and approaches, the quest for information empowers us to stay dexterous, versatile, and receptive to evolving conditions. Besides, ceaseless learning cultivates a culture of development inside associations, engaging workers to investigate groundbreaking thoughts, explore different avenues regarding new methodologies, and push the limits of what's conceivable.

Besides, nonstop learning empowers us to remain on top of things in a quickly developing market. In the present computerized economy, abilities become old at a remarkable rate, and the capacity to learn and adjust rapidly is fundamental for remaining applicable and employable. By putting resources into constant learning, we can future-verify our vocations and position ourselves for outcomes despite vulnerability and interruption.

Besides, persistent learning encourages a development mentality—aa conviction that our capacities can be created through devotion and difficult work. By embracing a development outlook, we can conquer difficulties, quickly return from disappointment, and accomplish our maximum capacity. This attitude of strength and steadiness is fundamental for driving advancement, as it urges us to face challenges, explore different avenues regarding groundbreaking thoughts, and gain from the two triumphs and disappointments enroute.

All in all, the significance of nonstop learning couldn't possibly be more significant in an advanced age. By focusing on deep-rooted learning, we can remain on top of things, stay pertinent and cutthroat in our vocations, and drive development inside our associations. Allow us to embrace the excursion of ceaseless advancement as a pathway to individual and expert development and as an impetus for making a superior future for us and for a long time into the future.

Significance of Nonstop Learning:

In the steadily advancing scene of advancement, one consistent part remains: the significance of nonstop learning. As we finish up our investigation of development in the computerized age, it turns out to be progressively evident that outcomes in this powerful climate depend on our capacity to adjust, advance, and procure new information and abilities. Hence, let us perceive the basics of deep-rooted learning and concede to an excursion of consistent development and improvement.

Development flourishes with interest, imagination, and a hunger for information. By developing an outlook of deep-rooted learning, we can encourage these fundamental characteristics inside ourselves and our associations, opening new doors and driving significant change. Allow us to embrace a feeling of interest, continually searching out groundbreaking thoughts, viewpoints, and experiences that challenge our presumptions and grow our viewpoints.

Also, let us perceive that learning isn't restricted to formal schooling or organized preparation programs. While these are significant instruments for gaining information and abilities, genuine learning happens through experience, trial and error, and reflection. Allow us to embrace a culture of trial and error and embrace disappointment as a characteristic and fundamental piece of the growing experience. By empowering ourselves as well as other people to face challenges, investigate novel thoughts, and gain from our slip-ups, we can establish a climate where advancement twists and development flourishes.

Besides, let us influence the force of innovation to work with learning and coordinated effort in new and imaginative ways. From online courses and virtual learning stages to web-based entertainment and computerized networks, innovation has democratized access to information and opened new doors for learning and system administration. Allow us to embrace these apparatuses and use them to interface with others, share thoughts, and team up on projects that drive advancement and make us feel valued.

All in all, let us perceive that the journey of development is one of nonstop learning and development. By embracing a mentality of deep-rooted getting the hang of, cultivating a culture of trial and error and reflection, and utilizing the force of innovation to work with learning and coordinated effort, we can open new doors, drive significant change, and make a superior future for us and ages to come.

Obligation to Advancement:

As we continue our investigation of the development of the computerized age, let us reaffirm our obligation to advancement as the main thrust for progress and flourishing. Development isn't just a popular expression or a passing pattern; it is the backbone of associations and social orders, filling development, driving seriousness, and empowering us to handle the most squeezing difficulties confronting our reality.

Allow us to invest in encouraging a culture that values qualities and focuses on development at each level of our associations. From the C-suite to the bleeding edges, let us enable representatives to think innovatively, face challenges, and seek after intense thoughts that can possibly change our organizations and ventures. Allow us to establish conditions where trial and error is supported, disappointment is embraced as a valuable open door, and achievement is commended as an aggregate accomplishment.

Besides, let us perceive that development isn't the obligation of a limited handful, but rather a common undertaking that requires dynamic investment and cooperation, all things considered. Allow us to draw in with clients, accomplices, and networks to co-make arrangements that address their necessities and goals. Allow us to embrace variety and incorporation as drivers of development, perceiving that different points of view and encounters improve our comprehension and fuel our inventiveness.

Besides, let us focus on putting resources into the assets, abilities, and framework important to development. Whether it's through financing innovative work drives, giving preparation and advancement amazing open doors to representatives, or encouraging associations with outer colleagues, let us focus on ventures that empower us to remain at the forefront of development and adjust to changing business sector elements.

All in all, let us embrace the test of development with mental fortitude, conviction, and assurance. By conceding to cultivating a culture of development, drawing in with partners, and putting resources into the assets and capacities important to drive significant change, we can open new doors, make an incentive for clients and partners, and fabricate a superior future for a long time into the future. Through our aggregate endeavors, we have the ability to shape a world that is more creative, comprehensive, and reasonable for all.